ïained

Kathy Burke

Level 3

Series Editors: Andy Hopkins and Jocelyn Potter

**Pearson Education Limited**
Edinburgh Gate, Harlow,
Essex CM20 2JE, England
and Associated Companies throughout the world.

**Pack** ISBN: 978-1-4058-5212-8
**Book** ISBN: 978-1-4058-5068-1
**CD-ROM** ISBN: 978-1-4058-5067-4

First edition published 2003
This edition published 2007

1 3 5 7 9 10 8 6 4 2

Text copyright © Kathy Burke 2003
This edition copyright © Pearson Education Ltd 2007
Illustrations by Horacio Domingues, map on page 9 by Witmor

Set in 11/13pt A. Garamond
Printed in China
SWTC/01

Produced for the Publishers by AC Estudio Editorial S.L.

Published by Pearson Education Ltd in association with Penguin Books Ltd,
both companies being subsidiaries of Pearson Plc

**Acknowledgements**
We are grateful to the following for permission to reproduce photographs:
**Eddie Brazil**: page 31; **Fortean Picture Library**: page 1, page 11, page 17, page 21 (t), page 21 (b), page 25,
page 27, page 30, page 36, page 37; **Getty Images**: page 19 (b); **Graphic Maps** page 9; **RIA Novosti Photo
Library**: page 39, **Robert Harding Photo Library**: page 16, page 18, page 19 (t); **Science Photo Library**:
page 3 (t), page 3 (b); **Topfoto**: page 13(t), page 13 (b); **Uri Geller Gallery**: page 24.

Every effort has been made to trace the copyright holders and we apologise in advance for any
unintentional omissions. We would be pleased to insert the appropriate
acknowledgement in any subsequent edition of this publication.

For a complete list of the titles available in the Penguin Active Reading series please write to your local
Pearson Longman office or to: Penguin Readers Marketing Department, Pearson Education,
Edinburgh Gate, Harlow, Essex CM20 2JE, England.

# Contents

|  |  |  |
|---|---|---|
|  | Activities 1 | iv |
| Chapter 1 | Other Worlds | 1 |
|  | Activities 2 | 6 |
| Chapter 2 | Strange Disappearances | 8 |
| Chapter 3 | Mysterious Monsters | 11 |
|  | Activities 3 | 14 |
| Chapter 4 | Ancient Worlds | 16 |
|  | Activities 4 | 22 |
| Chapter 5 | Mind and Body | 24 |
|  | Activities 5 | 28 |
| Chapter 6 | Ghosts and Past Lives | 30 |
|  | Activities 6 | 34 |
| Chapter 7 | Earth Mysteries | 36 |
|  | Talk about it | 40 |
|  | Write about it | 41 |
|  | Project: True Story? | 42 |

## 1.1 What's the book about?

1 **Look at the front cover of this book and discuss these questions.**

    **a** What can you see on the cover that is strange or unusual?

    **b** What do you think the book is about? Is it fact or fiction?

2 **Check the meaning of the these words in your dictionary. Then use them in the sentences and write possible answers to the questions.**

| aliens | giant | monster | power | predict |
|--------|-------|---------|-------|---------|

    **a** When he saw the sea ..........monster.......... , he was very frightened.

    Why was it frightening? ...........................................................................

    **b** The president has a lot of ................................... .

    What can a president do? ...........................................................................

    **c** ................................... come from other worlds.

    How do they travel? ...................................................................................

    **d** Some people can ................................... the future.

    What do they use to do this? .....................................................................

    **e** I saw a ................................... footprint on the beach.

    What made the footprint? ..........................................................................

## 1.2 What happens first?

**Discuss these questions and make notes. Look at the picture on page 1. What can you see? What is happening? What is going to happen?**

Notes

# CHAPTER 1

# Other Worlds

*He saw the machine disappearing into the sky. All the plants on that piece of ground were dead.*

When you look up into the night sky, what are you thinking? Do you believe that there are other worlds out there? Is there life in those worlds? Is it like life on Earth?

## ● What's out there?

Space is perhaps the most exciting mystery – the last big adventure. Governments have spent millions of pounds trying to discover its secrets.

So are the stories of **alien**s and **UFO**s true? There have been thousands of reports from ordinary people. But space travellers say that they have also seen UFOs. When *Apollo 11* made the first famous landing on the moon on 21 July 1969, the spacemen were not alone. Neil Armstrong and Buzz Aldrin saw 'two very large mysterious things' with bright lights. 'They are watching us,' Armstrong reported. This information was kept secret for years by the US government. But there have been many more reports of UFOs from space travellers and pilots of aeroplanes.

Have UFOs and aliens visited Earth? Many people say that they have seen them. Some people have taken photographs. Here are some of their stories.

**alien** /ˈeɪliən/ (n/adj) a living thing, perhaps a person, from another world
**UFO** /ˌjuː ef ˈəʊ/ (n) a mysterious thing in the sky, perhaps flying to Earth from another world

## ● Mysterious visitors

### Socorro, New Mexico, US, 1964

Policeman Lonnie Zamora was driving home when he saw a fire in the hills. Was it a car accident? As he drove nearer, he saw a large, egg-shaped 'machine' about five metres long. It had four legs and no windows or doors. Two very short 'men' were standing by it. Zamora knew they weren't from Earth. The machine suddenly made a loud noise and left the ground. Fire poured from it. It stayed silently in the air for a few minutes. Then it disappeared into the sky.

When more policemen arrived, Zamora's face was white with fear. Trees in the area were burning and the ground looked strange – like glass. There were four holes in the ground from the four legs. UFO **expert**s believe Zamora's story. He was usually a very calm person. There were also other reports of a strange thing of this description in the sky that night.

### Valensole, France, 1965

Farmer Maurice Masse saw two very short, strange 'men' in his field. They were standing by a strange-looking machine. When he came closer, they pointed a long stick at him. A light came from it, throwing him to the ground. He couldn't move. After some time he was able to sit up. He saw the machine disappearing into the sky. All the plants on that piece of ground were dead.

After this, Masse felt very tired for weeks. When UFO experts asked him questions, they showed him a painting of a UFO. His face went white. 'Where did you see my machine?' he asked. It was a painting of the UFO that policeman Zamora saw the year before in New Mexico.

### The green children

In the 1100s, a boy and a girl were found near the village of Woolpit in England. They were completely green. They didn't know where they were. They didn't speak the local language and only ate green vegetables. The boy soon died, but the girl began to eat the local food and lost her green colour. She learnt the language and talked about her life. In her world, all the people were green. One day, the sun became very bright and the air temperature changed. She and her brother fell asleep and then woke up in this new place.

expert /ˈeksp3ːt/ (n) someone who knows a lot about a subject

2

## ● Roswell

The Roswell crash happened many years ago, but it is still one of the most important and famous of the UFO stories. People started to ask questions: Have aliens really landed on Earth? Are governments hiding important information from us? Roswell began the great interest in UFOs. Hundreds of books and famous films like *The X-Files* have followed.

Roswell is a town in the US state of New Mexico. It was just another small, unimportant town until July 1947.

A farmer, William ('Mac') Brazel, was checking his fields after a terrible storm and found many pieces of metal. He thought they were from a plane crash. So he reported the crash to the police. He also took some of the metal for them to look at. The police passed the information to **the military**. They tested the metal and made a discovery. They couldn't break it or burn it. There was also strange writing on it in a language that no one could understand. They decided that the metal wasn't from Earth. In their opinion, it was from a UFO.

The military then reported the UFO crash to the local radio station. People were very interested and visited the crash area. The newspapers quickly printed this exciting story and soon people everywhere knew about Roswell.

**the military** /ðə ˈmɪlətəri/ (n/adj) the people in a country who fight in wartime; *military* planes are used for war

But after a few weeks, the military's report changed. The metal in the field wasn't from a UFO; it was from a military plane. They immediately closed the crash area, but they continued to take things away. For many years after this, the US government refused to say anything about the crash.

In 1994, the military told a new story. The pieces of metal weren't parts of a military plane. They came from special equipment for spying on the Soviet Union. Many people don't believe this story. They think that the government is keeping important information about UFOs from us. There have been many stories about small aliens who were found in the area around the crash in 1947 – some alive and some dead. In 1995, the military showed a film from the time of the crash. In the film, there was an examination of the body of a small alien by military doctors. But other people don't believe that this is true.

For years, experts have tried to find out what really happened at Roswell. But many important government papers have disappeared, so we will probably never know the true story.

## ● They took us away!

*There have been thousands of reports of aliens taking people onto UFOs. Are these stories true? Were the people dreaming? UFO experts believe some of the stories.*

• In 1961, Betty and Barney Hill were driving from Canada to New Hampshire, in the US, when they saw a light in the sky. It followed them until they stopped. They saw a large, yellow thing. Through a window, they could see strange 'people' inside. Mrs Hill was frightened, so her husband started driving again. Then they suddenly felt very tired.

The Hills woke up an hour later in a different place – fifty-six kilometres away. How did they get there? What happened in the missing hour? Later, they had terrible dreams about aliens, so they told their story to the military. Doctors asked them questions. Slowly, they began to remember what happened. They were taken onto the UFO by aliens. Alien 'doctors' examined them. They also gave them information about the position of different stars. Scientists agreed that this information was correct.

• In 1975, Travis Walton was working with other men in a forest when they saw a UFO. A green light pulled Travis up into the UFO. It then disappeared. When Travis was found five days later, he couldn't remember anything. He was much thinner and his arm was cut.

• In November 1989, a woman phoned the police with a strange report. Aliens were flying with a woman in the sky. Then two New York policemen reported the same thing! They saw a woman 'flying' out of a twelfth floor window. There were 'little people' flying around her. The aliens took her up into a UFO. The UFO then quickly flew away.

## 2.1 Were you right?

Look back at your notes in Activity 1.2. Then use these words in the sentences.

| aliens | another | ground | inside | strange | UFO |
|--------|---------|--------|--------|---------|-----|

1 On page 1 there is a picture of a UFO flying above the ..........ground.......... It
   has come from ................................. world.

2 On page 2, the policeman is looking at a UFO and two ................................. . The
   aliens are very ................................. , so the policeman is frightened.

3 On page 3 the man is looking at a large ................................. with strange people
   inside it. His wife is telling him to get into the ................................. .

## 2.2 What more did you learn?

1 Complete the table with information from Chapter 1.

| Name | They saw | Date | Place |
|------|----------|------|-------|
| Lonnie Zamora | | | |
| | | | Valensole, France |
| | | 1947 | |
| Betty and Barney Hill | | | |

2 Put these happenings at Roswell into the right order, 1–8 .

a ☐ The military test the metal. They think it is from a UFO.

b ☐ The military show a film of a small alien.

c ☐ William Brazel reports the metal pieces to the police.

d ☐ The police report the metal to the military.

e ☐1 There is a bad storm.

f ☐ The military say the metal is from spying equipment.

g ☐ The military say the metal is from a military plane.

h ☐ William Brazel sees pieces of metal in his fields.

## 2.3 Language in use

**Look at the sentence on the right. Then complete the sentences below using past continuous and past simple verb forms.**

> Lonnie Zamora **was driving** home when he **saw** a fire in the hills.

When the policeman ......*arrived*...... (arrive), ...................................... ...................................... (burn).

When the UFO ...................................... (disappear), ...................................... ...................................... (sit) on the ground.

William Brazel ...................................... (check) his fields when ...................................... ...................................... ...................................... (find).

Betty and Barney Hill ............................... ...................................... (drive) to New Hampshire when ...................... ...................................... (see).

## 2.4 What's next?

**In Chapter 2, you will read about strange disappearances. What do you think these are? Circle a possible answer.**

1  The Bermuda Triangle is a        place.    ship.    plane.

2  The *Mary Celeste* is a          place.    ship.    plane.

3  Atlantis is a                    place.    ship.    plane.

# Strange Disappearances

*They found an empty ship! Food, equipment and clothes
were all still there – but no people.*

Unexplained disappearances aren't new. All over the world, people or things
have disappeared for no reason. We still don't know why.

### ● The Bermuda Triangle

The Bermuda **Triangle** is an area of the Atlantic Ocean near the coast of Florida,
in the US. This area is famous for the disappearance of hundreds of ships and
planes. Stories like the two below have given experts some information about
this mystery.

• On 5 December 1945, five military planes were flying near the coast of
Florida. Suddenly, the pilots didn't know where they were. One of the pilots
phoned with these words: 'We seem to be lost ... Everything is wrong ... We can't
be sure of anything ... Our equipment has stopped working ... Even the ocean
doesn't look right ... ' Then the phone went dead. The planes were never seen
again. More than a hundred ships searched for them, but they were never found.

**triangle** /ˈtraɪæŋɡəl/ (n) a shape with three sides

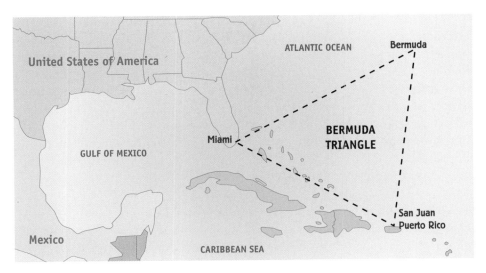

• On 11 June 1986, Martin Caidin was flying in good weather through a clear blue sky. Suddenly, the sky around the plane became very cloudy. Then it changed to bright yellow. It was so bright that Caidin couldn't see. His equipment 'went crazy' and stopped working. Above the plane, there was a hole and he could see blue sky through it. Below the plane, there was another hole. He could see the ocean at the of it. Caidin stayed calm and flew the plane for four hours. When he finally got back into blue sky, the plane's equipment immediately started working again. He looked back but he could only see clear blue sky.

Many ships have also disappeared in the Bermuda Triangle. People have tried to explain this mystery, but they have different opinions:
  – It is the perfect place for alien activity.
  – The lost city of Atlantis pulls these ships and planes down under the sea.
  – The weather is unusual there.
  – These 'strange' disappearances are ordinary accidents.

But if these disappearances are ordinary, why haven't searchers ever found any pieces of the planes and ships? Why does equipment stop working? Why does the sky change colour?

### ● The *Mary Celeste*, 'The Ghost Ship'

One of the strangest mysteries of the sea is the disappearance of the people on the ship, the *Mary Celeste*. The ship left New York on 7 November 1872. Benjamin Spooner Briggs and his family, and seven other men, were sailing to Genoa, in Italy.

A British ship, the *Dei Gratia*, also left New York on that day. On 5 December, the *Dei Gratia* sailed near the *Mary Celeste*. Was the ship having problems? Some of the men from the *Dei Gratia* went on the *Mary Celeste* to find out. They found an empty ship! Food, equipment and clothes were all still there – but no people. The men found Briggs's notebook. Nothing strange was written in it, but there was no writing after 25 November.

Where was everyone? Why did they leave? Perhaps the other men killed Briggs. Perhaps a sea **monster** attacked the ship, or there was a terrible storm. But why did the ship look so tidy? People have tried to explain this mystery for over a hundred years.

### ● Ordinary people
*Here are some famous old stories of ordinary people who disappeared. Why did they disappear? Where did they go? No one has been able to answer these questions.*

### *David Lang*
On 23 September 1880, David Lang, a farmer, disappeared in front of his family and friends. He was walking across a field towards them waving 'hello'. Suddenly, he was gone. The area was searched for months but nothing was found. The family were very frightened. But Mrs Lang refused to move her family away until her husband was found.

Seven months later, while she was playing, their daughter heard her father crying for help. She found a circle of dead grass in the place where he was seen for the last time. She screamed for her mother and Mrs Lang ran to her daughter. She saw the circle of dead grass, but she couldn't hear her husband. This frightened her again, and she moved her family to another town.

### *The Vaughan children*
In 1906, three young children disappeared while they were playing in a field near their home. Searches quickly began, but after three days the children were still missing. On the morning of the fourth day, a farm worker found them lying asleep on the ground.

The children were clean, and they weren't hungry or frightened, but they didn't remember anything. They were very surprised that everyone was looking for them. They could only remember waking up. For the rest of their lives, the children didn't know what happened to them during those three days.

**monster** /ˈmɒnstə/ (n) a large, ugly, frightening animal

# CHAPTER 3

# Mysterious Monsters

*The next morning, he saw large footprints in the snow. They were thirty-five centimetres long and eighteen centimetres wide.*

*There are many strange living things on land and in the sea that are still a mystery. Some of them seem to come from another time. Some aren't often seen or photographed. But enough people say that they have seen them. As a result, we want to find out more.*

### ● The Loch Ness monster

'Nessie', the Loch Ness monster, is probably the most famous lake monster in the world. There are well-known lake monsters in Canada, the US, Sweden, Norway, Iceland and other countries. But Nessie feels like part of the family to many of us because we have known about her for so long.

The first description of a monster in Loch Ness, Scotland, was more than 400 years ago. There have been many reports since then. Some of these have been honest mistakes. But sometimes people have lied to make money from the Nessie story. No one has proved that a monster really lives in Loch Ness. But some people have taken good photographs. Experts and ordinary people have watched the lake for years. They are still trying to explain the mystery. Many tourists come each year to try to see the monster. 'Nessie watchers' travel to Scotland to look for her. Since 1930, more than 3,000 people have reported seeing the Loch Ness monster.

The first newspaper story about Nessie was in 1933. Mrs Mackay was driving along the lake when she saw something moving in the water. It was a very large, black animal and it was moving up and down. Her report gave a lot of information.

Then, in 1934, Dr Kenneth Wilson took one of the most famous black and white photographs of Nessie. There wasn't a better photograph until 1977. In that year, Doc Shiels took some colour photographs of the monster while he was on holiday. Some of these photos were lost or destroyed. This has often happened. People have broken or lost their cameras – and sometimes important photographs, too! It's part of the mystery.

Many scientists agree that there is 'some kind of living thing' in the lake. This 'thing' is very large and has a long neck. But no one has *proved* yet that a monster lives in Loch Ness.

### ● Don't go in the water!

You are lying on a beautiful beach, looking at the lovely blue water ... But what is under the water, deep down in that terrible black world? Some people feel that sea monsters are the most frightening of all monsters. In Herman Melville's book *Moby Dick*, a fisherman fought a long, bloody war with a terrible **whale**. When Steven Spielberg's film *Jaws* was first shown, people of all ages screamed in cinemas around the world.

But sea monsters aren't only in films and books. People have discovered 'real' monsters in the seas and oceans. These are often more frightening than a monster from a story.

### *Giant squid*

The idea of a **giant squid** is very frightening, but people have seen them. A US military ship was sailing near Newfoundland, Canada, when suddenly a very large whale jumped out of the water. It was fighting with a giant squid. The whale looked about eighteen metres long, but the squid was trying to kill it with its long arms. The squid was as big as the whale! The men on the ship were very frightened. They didn't want to get close enough to take photographs. These giant squid are true monsters. It still isn't understood why they grow so large.

### *The 'Globster'*

This is probably the most unusual monster. In November 1922, people on a beach in South Africa watched two whales fighting with a sea monster. The fight continued for hours. The monster sometimes jumped six metres out of the water and hit the whales with its tail. The whales won the fight and swam away.

---

**whale** /weɪl/ (n) a very large animal that swims in the sea; it takes in air through a hole on the top of its head
**giant** /ˈdʒaɪənt/ (adj) very, very large
**squid** /skwɪd/ (n) a sea animal with a long, soft body and ten arms

The dead monster was then pushed onto the beach by the water. People couldn't believe what they saw. It was a very large, shapeless thing, with a long neck and no head! It was fourteen metres long, three metres wide and one and a half metres high. No expert could name the animal. Many people, often fishermen, have reported seeing these large, ugly monsters.

## ● Monsters that walk the Earth

There are monsters in mountains and wild areas. Many people have seen monsters in China, Nepal, Russia, North America and other places that are 'half man and half animal'. No one has ever caught one. Here are the two most famous of these monsters.

### The Yeti

'Yeti' have walked in the Himalayan mountains of Nepal and China for hundreds of years. Reports from climbers in the Himalayan mountains have described them as very tall – nearly three metres. A Yeti stands like a man and has hair all over its body. It is dangerous and can attack people. Most people have seen signs of the Yeti in the snow. These have the shape of a man's foot but are very large. They can't be the feet of an animal.

The most famous report came from Don Whillans, a British climber, in 1970. In the mountains of Nepal, he watched a Yeti playing in the snow by the light of the moon for about twenty minutes. The next morning, he saw large footprints in the snow. They were thirty-five centimetres long and eighteen centimetres wide.

### Bigfoot

'Bigfoot' is the American 'Yeti'. The Native Americans* first saw the monster and named it *Sasquatch*. Reports of Bigfoot have continued since the early 1900s. Descriptions are similar to descriptions of the Yeti.

The most frightening story came from Albert Ostman, a Canadian, in 1924. A large, strange-looking animal picked him up and carried him for three hours.

* Native Americans: the first people in North America, before Europeans arrived

### 3.1 Were you right?

**Look back at Activity 2.4. Then tick (✓) the right answers.**

1 ☐ The Bermuda Triangle is a place near New York.

2 ☐ The Bermuda Triangle is a place near Florida.

3 ☐ Atlantis is a place, a lost city under the sea.

4 ☐ Atlantis is a place, a town in Italy.

5 ☐ The *Mary Celeste* is the name of a plane.

6 ☐ The *Mary Celeste* is the name of a ship.

### 3.2 What more did you learn?

1 **Match the first part of these sentences about the Bermuda Triangle with their endings.**

| | | | |
|---|---|---|---|
| 1 | Five military planes disappeared | **a** | ... through a hole in the cloud. |
| 2 | The pilots had no idea | **b** | ... near the coast of Florida. |
| 3 | Ships searched for them, | **c** | ... but they were never found. |
| 4 | When Martin Caidin flew there, | **d** | ... the sky turned yellow. |
| 5 | He could only see blue sky | **e** | ... he could only see clear sky. |
| 6 | Looking back later, | **f** | ... since then. |
| 7 | A lot of ships have disappeared | **g** | ... where they were |

2 **Match the monster with the place. Write the letter.**

| A Nepal and China | B South Africa | C North America | D Scotland | E Canada |
|---|---|---|---|---|

1 ☐ Nessie     2 ☐ Giant squid     3 ☐ Globster

4 ☐ Yeti     5 ☐ Bigfoot

## 3.3 Language in use

**Look at the sentence on the right. Then use** *many, more, most* **or** *the most* **in these sentences.**

> 'Nessie' ... is probably **the most** famous lake monster in the world.

1   There are lake monsters in ..................many.................. countries.

2   Dr Wilson took one of ............................................. famous photographs of Nessie.

3   A giant squid is ............................................. frightening than a whale.

4   The globster is probably ............................................. unusual monster.

5   ............................................. fishermen have seen globsters.

6   ............................................. signs of Yeti are footprints in the snow.

7   ............................................. frightening story about Bigfoot came from Albert Ostman in 1924.

## 3.4 What's next?

**Look at the pictures on pages 16–19. Discuss what you know about these places. Then write about them below. What do you think the story is about? Make notes.**

**Stonehenge** ....................................................................................................................

....................................................................................................................

....................................................................................................................

....................................................................................................................

**Easter Island**....................................................................................................................

....................................................................................................................

....................................................................................................................

....................................................................................................................

**The Pyramids of Giza** ....................................................................................................

....................................................................................................................

....................................................................................................................

....................................................................................................................

**The Giant Sphinx** ..........................................................................................................

....................................................................................................................

....................................................................................................................

....................................................................................................................

# CHAPTER 4

# Ancient Worlds

*But before the year ended, twelve of the twenty scientists
from his team were dead!*

W*e are learning about new mysteries every day. There are reports of alien
activity, strange new 'monsters', unexplained stories in medicine, strange
activity in space. It seems that the number of mysteries is growing. Or are we
just more interested? Examples of mysteries come from the early days of our life
on earth.*

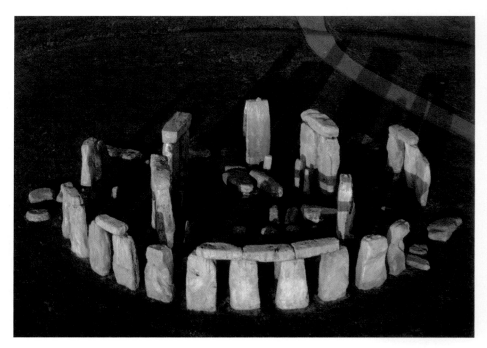

## ● How did they do it?

### *Stonehenge*

Stonehenge, in the UK, is different from anything of its kind in Europe. After
5,000 years, it is still standing. But why was it built? Was Stonehenge used like
a giant computer to make **predict**ions from the position of the sun, moon and
stars? This is the most popular opinion.

*How* was it built? Many of the heavy stones were brought from 240
kilometres away, so 1,500 men had to work every day for over five years, in one

**predict** /prɪˈdɪkt/ (v) to say that something will happen

expert's opinion. The very large top stones fit into the smaller standing stones. This needed tools and skills that people didn't have at that time. Experts agree that a higher intelligence was needed. So who built Stonehenge? No one knows. For this reason, it is still one of the world's most interesting mysteries.

### *The Easter Island statues*

The island of Rapa Nui, in the Pacific Ocean, was named Easter Island when it was 'discovered' by Europeans on Easter Day in 1722. It is famous for over 800 stone **statue**s, called *moai*. The statues are between one and ten metres tall and have similar faces. They stand by the sea, facing the land.

Why did the people of Easter Island build them? Some experts think that the statues were the 'homes' of **ghost**s of people from the island's past. The ghosts looked through the statues' eyes and guarded the island. People built the statues and then moved them to another part of the island (twenty-five kilometres away) and put them on platforms. In the early 1990s, forty scientists moved fifteen of the statues and put them on new platforms. They used modern equipment and worked every day, but it took them four years. So how did the people of Easter Island move more than 300 statues? Scientists have found no answers.

**statue** /ˈstætʃuː/ (n) something (in stone or metal, for example) that looks like a person or animal
**ghost** /ɡəʊst/ (n) a frightening, moving thing in the shape of a person who has died

## ● Mysteries of Egypt

### *The Pyramids*

The three most famous Egyptian **pyramid**s are in Giza. They were built for the bodies of the pharaohs* after they died almost 5,000 years ago. The pharaohs' gold was put with them for the 'next life'. The Great Pyramid is the largest. It is 140 metres high and 228 metres wide at its widest point. King Khufu's body is there. People think that the pyramid shape helped the pharaohs climb to the sky after their death. So how were the pyramids built? That is still not known. Scientists think that over 100,000 men worked for more than twenty years to build the Great Pyramid. More than two million stones were used. The stones were very large and very heavy. How were they lifted to the top?

* pharaohs: the kings of Egypt

**pyramid** /'pɪrəmɪd/ (n) an old stone building with walls that meet at a single point at the top

### *The Great Sphinx*

The Sphinx guards the pyramids. It is twenty metres high and more than seventy-three metres long. The face is four metres high and each eye is nearly two metres long. The Sphinx has the head of King Khufu's son, King Khafre. The body of an animal shows how strong the king was. Experts still can't explain how it was built.

### *King Tutankhamen*

The Valley of the Kings is near the city of Luxor, in Egypt. The bodies of the most famous pharaohs were put in special rooms there. An Englishman, Howard Carter, searched for years for the place where King Tutankhamen's body was kept. In 1923, he found a large room filled with gold and other beautiful things. He took many things away. But Carter and his team paid a terrible price for their discovery. A sign at the entrance promised death to the people who opened it. Carter didn't believe this. But before the year ended, twelve of the twenty scientists from his team were dead!

*Were there really 'perfect' **civilizations** thousands of years ago? Were the people beautiful and intelligent? Did they live without war? Were their lives more wonderful than we can imagine? Or is this just our hope for a perfect world?*

## ● Lost civilizations

The Greek writer Plato told a story about an island in the Atlantic Ocean called Atlantis. It was a beautiful place. The people were intelligent and had many interests. The land was rich with plant and animal life. The people used their skills well, so the island was a centre for farming and business. Their buildings were beautiful and well built. Their kings and queens had great **power** in Europe and Africa. This was more than 11,000 years ago – and then the city disappeared under the sea.

Was there really an Atlantis? If there was, why did it disappear? Some experts agree on one idea: perhaps the story of Atlantis is really the story of the Greek island Santorini. People still want to know about Atlantis. They are still looking for this lost civilization.

**civilization** /ˌsɪvəlaɪˈzeɪʃən/ (n) a group of people who have the same laws and ordered way of life
**power** /ˈpaʊə/ (n) a strong position over people; they must do what they are told

There have also been reports about the **ancient** civilization of Mu, near Japan. There are photographs of this 'mystery city' under the sea. People believe they have seen buildings, statues and roads.

## ● The Nazca Lines

In Peru, very large 'drawings' of animals and 1,300 kilometres of straight lines cover more than 500 square kilometres of land. These were made by the Nazca people thousands of years ago. Scientists have travelled to Peru to study these shapes and lines. Many of the animal shapes are as big as two football fields. You can't see them from the ground because they are so large. So scientists have to take photographs from the air. There are many questions about the Nazca Lines. Why are they so large? How could the Nazca people make perfect shapes like these when they couldn't see them from the ground? Who or what were they made for? Perhaps they were used to predict the weather and the best time for planting **crop**s. Some people think the lines have a religious meaning.

ancient /ˈeɪnʃənt/ (adj) from a very long time ago
crop /krɒp/ (n) a plant, like rice or fruit, that you grow for food

## 4.1 Were you right?

Look back at your answers to Activity 3.4. Then complete the sentences about each picture.

> Easter Island    Great Sphinx    The Pyramids
> Nazca Lines    Atlantis    Stonehenge

**1** ............*Great Sphinx*............: a statue with the head of a man and the body of an animal.

**2** .........................................: a circle made from heavy stones.

**3** .........................................: an island under the sea.

**4** .........................................: a place with eight hundred statues.

**5** .........................................: animal shapes cut into the ground.

**6** .........................................: pointed buildings made from millions of stones.

## 4.2 What more did you learn?

Match the words with a possible 'speaker'.

**1** ☐ 'I am guarding the Pyramids.'

**2** ☐ 'I am going to write a story about Atlantis.'

**3** ☐ 'The ghosts of our grandparents live in the statues.'

**4** ☐ 'I want to take my gold with me when I die.'

**5** ☐ 'Twelve scientists died after we found the room.'

**4.3** **Language in use**

Look at the question on the right. Then make questions for these answers. Use passive verb forms.

> How **was** it **built?**

1  Who ........ *were the Pyramids built for* ............? (build)

   For the pharaohs.

2  What ...................................................? (guard)

   By the Sphinx.

3  Where ...................................................? (find)

   In the Valley of the Kings.

4  Who ...................................................? (make)

   By the Nazca people in Peru.

5  When ...................................................? (discover)

   In 1722, when Europeans arrived there.

6  Where ...................................................? (move)

   To platforms, in another part of the island.

**4.4** **What's next?**

Chapter 5 is about people who can do strange things with their minds and bodies. The sentences below tell you about some of these people. Discuss the best ending for each sentence.

1  Uri Geller changes

| A  about the future. |

2  Nostradamus wrote a book

| B  over fire. |

3  David Booth dreamed

| C  the shape of metal things. |

4  'I will die on my 45ᵗʰ birthday,'

| D  thought John Snell. |

5  Kuda Bux walked

| E  out of a third-floor window. |

6  Daniel Douglas Home flew

| F  about a plane crash. |

# Mind and Body

*He used the power of his mind to change the shape of
metal things like spoons, forks and keys.*

**W**e *know that our bodies aren't just simple machines. But what powers do
our minds have over our bodies? How can an ordinary man suddenly lift
a car to save someone's life? How do people walk on fire without feeling pain?
What is the mind? Science is still not sure.*

● **The power of the mind**
Uri Geller became famous in the
1970s. He used the power of his mind
to change the shape of metal things
like spoons, forks and keys. He has
shown his very unusual skills many
times. He can 'see' when his eyes are
covered. He can describe a picture
or 'read' a letter. He has stopped
clocks working. Geller discovered his
powers when he was only four years
old. Scientists still can't explain how
he does these things. Not everyone
believes in his powers. But no one has
proved that they aren't real.

● **Nostradamus**
Would you like to see into the future?
Do you know anyone who has this
power? The earliest known person
with this power was Michel Nostradame, 'Nostradamus' (1503–66). He had
great skill as a doctor and he was very brave. When the 'Black Death' killed
thousands of people in France in the 1500s, he saved many people. But he
couldn't save his wife and children from this terrible illness. When they died, he
left his home. He travelled around Europe and became interested in mysteries.
Other people soon discovered his power to predict the future. He became very
well known in Europe and wrote a famous book, *Les Propheties*, of more than
1,000 predictions. These predictions were about times that were 500 years into
the future.

Nostradamus correctly predicted many important things: the power of Hitler in Germany, the Second World War, and the deaths of some important people. He wrote of President Kennedy, 'His death will be sudden and sad.' Nostradamus even correctly predicted his own death. He described exactly how he would die. When something important happens in the world, experts still read his predictions. Other people with this power have become famous since Nostradamus's time, but Nostradamus's work still interests people after 500 years.

### ● Dreams of the future

Some people have a strange feeling (often a dream) that something – usually bad – is going to happen in the future. They can't explain the feeling but they are very sure. Many people have 'seen' terrible things that have happened in the world. They have known about them before they happened!

- A girl had a dream about the end of the great ship *Titanic* on the night that it happened. She saw a large ship with many people on it. Suddenly, she heard a loud scream and one end of the ship went up into the air. The ship then disappeared quickly into the sea. Ocean travel was dangerous in those days, but how can we explain stories like hers?
- In 1979, David Booth had the same dream night after night. In his dream, he saw a plane crashing and burning near buildings. He told people about his dream, but he couldn't give them the time or place. The next day, a plane crashed at Chicago Airport and everyone on the plane was killed.
- The night before the attacks on New York in September 2001, a woman dreamt that she met a friend in New York. He was crying and pointing to two tall buildings. They were burning. The next morning, the attacks happened.

- John Snell lived in Poole, in England. On holiday, he paid a woman to look into his future. She told him, 'You will die on your forty-fifth birthday.' He wasn't frightened because he didn't believe her. For twenty years, he worked long hours and enjoyed drinking. But as his forty-fifth birthday came nearer, he started to worry. He stopped drinking. On his birthday, he refused to go out. The next day, he read a local newspaper report about the death of John Snell of Poole on his forty-fifth birthday. The woman was right and wrong. There were *two* John Snells living in Poole. The other John Snell died!

## ● Body mysteries
*Some of these stories show the power of the mind over the body. Others show frightening things that have happened to people's bodies. All are mysteries.*

### Fire!
How can a person suddenly start burning for no reason? There have been many terrible examples of this. The person is burnt to death very quickly, but nothing around them is burnt.

Jacqueline Fitzsimmon, a seventeen-year-old student, was walking down the college stairs with two friends when she suddenly started burning. Three people tried to stop the fire, but it was too fast. She died in minutes. Firemen and police could find no reason for the fire or why it was so sudden.

### The 'light' woman
In April 1934, a young woman from Pirano in Italy began to have a very strange problem. When she was sleeping, a blue light came from her body. When she woke up, it disappeared. Her family called in scientists. The scientists watched her sleeping for a week, but they couldn't explain it. After three weeks, the blue light disappeared and never returned.

### Fire-walking

We have heard stories for many years about religious men walking on fire. In 1935, this was tested for the first time. An Indian man, Kuda Bux, walked over a fire. The fire's temperature was 300°C, but his feet weren't burnt and he felt no pain. Scientists watched and it was filmed. Scientists now agree that this is an example of the power of the mind over the body. In this photo a fire-walker in Sri Lanka walks calmly across hot stones.

### Up, up and away

Some people are able to lift themselves off the ground and stay in the air with no help. Most reports of this are about religious people. The most famous story from Europe is of an Englishman, Daniel Douglas Home. In 1868, while people watched, he 'flew' out of a third-floor window. He then flew back into the building through an open window in another room. Asian countries have many stories like this. A Tibetan religious man, Milarepa, slept, ate and walked in the air!

## 5.1 Were you right?

**Look back at Activity 4.4. Then answer these questions.**

1  Who can change the shape of metal things?  .................................................

2  Who wrote about the future?  .................................................

3  Who dreamed about a plane crash?  .................................................

4  Who walked over a fire?  .................................................

5  Who didn't die on his forty-fifth birthday?  .................................................

6  Who flew out of a third-floor window?  .................................................

## 5.2 What more did you learn?

**Circle the right answer.**

1  What has Uri Geller stopped working?

> Cars.  (Clocks.)  Computers.

2  What was The Black Death?

> An illness.  A book.  A prediction.

3  What was the *Titanic*?

> A building.  A ship.  A plane.

4  Which city was attacked in September 2001?

> Chicago.  London.  New York.

5  What did Jacqueline Fitzsimmon suddenly do?

> She walked.  She burnt to death.  She disappeared.

6  What came from the girl in Pirano's body when she was sleeping?

> A blue light.  Fire.  Water.

7  Who did her family ask to watch her?

> Doctors.  Policemen.  Scientists.

8  What happened to Kuda Bux's feet when he walked over fire?

> They hurt.  They turned white.  Nothing.

**5.3 Language in use**

Look at the sentence on the right.
Then choose a word from the box
to complete these sentences.

> He told people about his dream, **but** he
> couldn't give them a time or place.

| because | and | while | until | but | so |
|---|---|---|---|---|---|

1 Uri Geller can change the shape of metal things ............*and*............ can stop clocks
  working.

2 Nostradamus made his predictions 500 years ago ......................... people are still
  interested in his work.

3 John Snell wasn't frightened ......................... he didn't believe the prediction.

4 The firemen didn't arrive ......................... Jacqueline was dead.

5 Her family was worried about the blue light, ......................... they called in
  scientists.

6 Milorepa slept ......................... he was in the air.

**5.4 What's next?**

**Chapter 6 is about ghosts. Do you know of any famous ghosts, in real life or in
fiction?**

a Make notes about one ghost. Where was it seen?
  What was it like? What did it do?

Notes

b Compare your ghost with the ghosts of other students. Whose is the most
  interesting/frightening/amusing? Why?

# Ghosts and Past Lives

*She finally turned towards him, and she had no face.*
*He screamed and ran away.*

D*o you believe in ghosts? Can people really return to life on Earth after death?*

● **Ghost houses**

In 1863, a large house was built next to Borley Church, near the town of Bury St Edmunds. The house became famous because many strange things happened there. There were noises. Things flew through the air. Some people heard a person walking through the house. Ghosts were seen. The most famous ghost was a young woman; her ghost was often seen in the gardens.

In 1928, Lionel and Marianne Foyster moved into the house. Marianne

immediately hated the dark, ugly building. Soon after they moved in, frightening things began to happen. When a ghost wrote messages to Marianne on the walls, photographs were taken. Local people didn't believe Marianne's stories, but more than 2,000 mysterious things were reported during the Foysters' five-year stay.

When the house was destroyed in a fire in 1939, that seemed to be the end of the story. Then local people began to talk about strange things happening in Borley Church.

In 1974, the BBC filmed Borley Church. They put sound equipment inside and watched the church. They heard loud noises: people talking, a door opening and closing, heavy footsteps. But the door *didn't* open or close and they found no one. All the sound equipment in the church was destroyed. One night, two of the BBC filmmakers saw the ghost of the young woman in the garden. They watched her for twelve minutes! Denny Densham from the BBC said, 'I can't explain what I've seen at Borley.'

Since the BBC visit, many more mysterious things have happened at Borley Church. You can visit the church on your next trip to England if you are brave enough!

A house in Norfolk, England, is famous for the ghost called 'the Brown Lady'. She was first seen in 1835, very late at night. She wore a beautiful brown dress and her face shone with light. But she had no eyes – only two black holes! In 1936, two photographers from *Country Life* magazine came to take photographs of the house. They saw the Brown Lady moving up the stairs. They were very frightened, but they took this famous photograph. It is one of the best photographs of a ghost. Since this time nobody has seen the Brown Lady in the house. Did the photo frighten her away?

## ● Around the world

*Every country has famous ghosts and ghost stories. Some countries have similar ghosts but with different names. Do you have any of these ghosts in your country?*

### India

An *acheri* is the ghost of a little girl who lives in the mountains. She comes into the villages at night to make the children sick. Children wear pieces of red cotton round their necks to protect them from the *acheri*. In many European stories, people also wear red to protect themselves from bad ghosts.

## Japan

Japan has many ghosts. The *buruburu* is the 'ghost of fear'. It lives in dark forests and looks like a shaking old man or woman, often with one eye. The *buruburu* jumps on a person's back. The person suddenly feels very cold and dies of fear.

The 'faceless woman' was first seen in Tokyo hundreds of years ago. A man was walking home one night when he saw a woman crying. He tried to help her, but she couldn't stop crying. She finally turned towards him, and she had no face. He screamed and ran away. He ran until he saw an old man on the road. He told him about the woman's face. 'Was it like this?' asked the old man as he turned round. He, too, had no face!

## Germany

The word *poltergeist* comes from German and means 'noisy ghost'. How does a ghost become a poltergeist? Perhaps if a person dies in a terrible way, their ghost stays angry after their death. A poltergeist stayed in a man's office in Germany for a year. It destroyed furniture, threw things, turned lights on and off and moved pictures round the walls. It also made hundreds of expensive telephone calls. Experts discovered that it was angry with a secretary. When she moved away, the activity stopped.

## The Muslim world

The *zar* is known in Muslim countries. It is a man-hating ghost. It comes into a house and makes a wife crazy. As a result, she shouts at her husband all the time. There is only one way to send the *zar* away. The husband must be very kind to his wife and give her expensive presents!

## Russia

*Domoviks* live behind the cooker. When a family moves house, they welcome the *domovik* to his new home with a fire in the cooker. The *domovik* looks after the house. But if you make him angry, he will burn your house down.

A *rusalka* is the ghost of a young woman who has died in water. *Rusalkas* are beautiful, with long green hair. They live in lakes and rivers and secretly help poor, hard-working fishermen.

## ● Past lives

*Have you ever thought, 'I've been to this place before', or 'I've already met this person?' Here are some stories of people who lived complete lives in other times.*

### Bridey Murphy

Virginia Tighe was the wife of a businessman in Wisconsin, in the US. But this wasn't her only life. One hundred years before, she was a young Irish woman called Bridey Murphy. Virginia's story is one of the most famous in the world. Why have so many experts believed her? Virginia never travelled and knew nothing about Ireland, but she knew many important things about Bridey's life and town: the language, the names of local shops and people, the type of money, even popular songs. Experts have checked Virginia's story for over thirty years. They haven't proved that it isn't true.

### Shanti Devi

Shanti Devi was born in 1926 in Delhi, India. When she was four years old, she began to talk about her 'other life' as a wife and mother in the town of Mathura. She said things like, 'This was my husband's favourite food.' She remembered many things about her life in Mathura. Her husband wore glasses and had a clothes shop. She died when she had her second baby. At nine years old, Shanti remembered her husband's name: Pandit Kedarnath Chaube. Shanti's parents wrote to him and invited him to their house. Shanti knew him immediately. She then wanted to go back to her old home. Family and friends went with her. When they arrived in Mathura, she saw her husband's brother. She immediately knew who he was. She found her old house without help. She knew where her bedroom was. She found some of her things there. Pandit agreed that they were hers. Shanti's story interested people all over the world. Mahatma Gandhi invited her to his home. But Shanti always missed her first life and never married. She died sad and lonely.

### The Pollock children

In 1957, sadness came to the Pollock family of Hexham, England. The only children, two sisters, were killed by a car. The Pollocks found happiness again when Mrs Pollock had more children – two more girls. But something was strange about these children. They knew all about their dead sisters' lives. They knew about their school, their friends and even their toys. When the girls were older, their parents sometimes found them crying. When cars drove quickly along the road, they screamed. All of this stopped when the girls became older. After that, they couldn't remember any of it. Experts still can't say why these things happened to the Pollock children.

## 6.1 Were you right?

Look back at your answer to Activity 5.4. Read the story about the *buruburu* at the top of page 32 and compare it to your ghost. Are the two ghosts similar in any way?

| Similar | Different |
|---------|-----------|
|         |           |

## 6.2 What more did you learn?

**Answer the questions.**

**1** Why did the BBC go to Borley Church?

To make a film.

**2** What does an *acheri* do?

...............................................................................................

**3** What does a *poltergeist* do?

...............................................................................................

**4** Who was the poltergeist in the German office angry with?

...............................................................................................

**5** What does a *zar* do?

...............................................................................................

**6** What does a *domovik* do?

...............................................................................................

**7** Where do *rusalkas* live?

...............................................................................................

**8** Where was Virginia Tighe from in her first life?

...............................................................................................

**9** Why did Shanti Devi go to Mathura?

...............................................................................................

**10** What changed the lives of Mr and Mrs Pollock?

...............................................................................................

## 6.3 Language in use

Look at the question on the right.
Then make other questions using
present perfect verb forms.

> **Have you ever thought**, 'I've been to this place before?'

1   ...........*Have you seen*........... (you/see) a ghost?

2   ................................................. (there/be) a ghost in Borley Church?

3   ................................................. (anyone/take) a photograph of the Brown Lady?

4   ................................................. (you/live) before, do you think?

5   ................................................. (they/welcome) the *domovik* to their house?

6   ................................................. (her husband/send) the *zar* away?

## 6.4 What happens next?

Discuss what happened to the people in these pictures.

# CHAPTER 7

# Earth Mysteries

*Suddenly, a very large ball of fire covered most of
the sky. Then everything went black.*

The Earth has its own great mysteries. Science has still not explained many of
the strange things that have happened to our weather, land and animals.

### ● Crop circles

In the early 1980s, strange things started happening on English farms. There
were many reports of large circles in fields. Crops were flattened, but they were
still growing. The circles had beautiful shapes inside. The first crop circles were
seen on small farms. They didn't become well known until later in the 1980s.

When more crop circles were seen, scientists were called in. They were very
interested in the beautiful shapes. The shapes weren't simple. Some experts
thought that perhaps they were made by an 'unknown intelligence' – by aliens.
Many of the circles were found near ancient places like Stonehenge. This added
to the interest in aliens. But other scientists disagreed. They thought they were
made by strange winds.

By the end of the 1980s, crop circles were very famous. But were they made by aliens or winds, or were people just playing games? Some people thought that the shapes were an ancient language. They 'read' predictions in the circles.

In 1990, many more crop circles were reported, with some of the most beautiful shapes. People from other countries came to England to see them. Filmmakers waited in fields at night and tried to film the circle-making. But they were never able to see it – only the finished circles. Crop circles were a bigger mystery than ever. Who was making them? How were they making them? And why?

In 1990, it was discovered that ordinary people were making some of the circles. Two of these people were artists, Doug Bower and Dave Chorley. Their circles were called the 'Doug and Dave' circles. Experts wanted to be sure that people really could make these. £15,000 was offered to the person who could make the best crop circle. Some beautiful shapes were produced. This proved that ordinary people could make crop circles. Many experts lost interest then.

But every year, new crop circles are seen. Many 'crop circle makers' can't explain some of these new shapes. They are so perfect – too difficult to draw on paper. How can someone make these beautiful shapes in the short summer night? Why hasn't anyone ever seen a person making a crop circle? The mystery continues.

## ● Other mysteries

*In some of the stranger Earth mysteries, surprising things fall from the sky or come out of the ground. Sometimes there is a sudden unexplainable change in the weather. There are many more stories like these, but not many answers!*

### *It's raining!*

• In 1985, in Texas, small fish fell into a man's back garden. When he went outside, hundreds more living fish fell out of the sky.

- Thousands of **frog**s fell during heavy storms in Birmingham, England in 1954, in Canet-Plage, France in 1977 and in Arkansas, US in 1973.
- In England in 1987, sand rained from the sky four times. Scientists tested the sand. They discovered that it was from the Sahara!

### Animals in stone
In 1960, workers were breaking stones when they found small frogs inside – some living and some dead. One scientist said, 'They've probably been in the rocks for thousands of years. Some of their mouths have grown shut.' People could see their hearts moving through their thin skins. Scientists can't explain why some of the frogs were still alive.

### Strange lights
In January 1984, a 'ball of light' flew through a Russian plane, above the frightened passengers. It then broke into two parts, formed a ball again and suddenly disappeared.

Ghost lights are moving balls of light that change colour. They are only seen away from cities. They disappear if you go near them. Many people think they are ghosts. They are only seen in places where people have died in terrible ways. Reports of these strange lights have come from Britain, the US and Japan.

### Weather changes
- At 7.30 a.m. on 7 July 1987, the temperature in the American town of Greensburg, Kansas went up 11°C in ten minutes – from 24°C to 35°C. No one has found a reason for this.
- In March 1978, workers in a field in France heard a very loud noise and the earth shook. The noise came from the next field. They ran to the field and found a very large hole in the ground. In the hole was a 25-kilo piece of ice. The ice stayed in one piece for an hour.

## ● The Siberian mystery
In the early morning of 30 June 1908, a very large ball of fire came from the sky and hit the Tunguska river valley in Siberia. In seconds, everything for sixty-five kilometres was destroyed. Farmer Sergei Semenov was eighty kilometres away, but he saw a very large light in the sky and felt terrible heat. It almost burnt his shirt off his back. Suddenly, a very large ball of fire covered most of the sky. Then everything went black.

---

**frog** /frɒg/ (n) a small green animal that lives near water; frogs have long legs for jumping

When scientists visited the Tunguska valley after this, they couldn't believe their eyes. Dead 'cooked' animals were still standing. There were no living trees or plants of any kind. The Tunguska river was boiling hot. Later, it was reported that people seventy kilometres away were thrown into the air. Scientists have tried to find out why this happened for almost a hundred years. It is still one of the world's greatest Earth mysteries.

### ● It's all a mystery

Some scientists think Tunguska happened as a result of a 'black hole'. Black holes are formed from stars that are much larger than our sun. The centre of the star is pressed until it breaks. In less than a second, it becomes a 'black hole'.

What happens then? Some experts think that black holes are the reason for some of the Earth's strange disappearances in places like the Bermuda Triangle. One thing is sure; black holes are the greatest mystery of space and time.

We are discovering more and more about our world. But as we learn more, we have more questions. Many things about this world are still a mystery...

**1** Answer these questions yourself. Then ask ten or more other people. Write their names.

Do you believe in ...?

aliens

UFOs

monsters

ghosts

**2** Work with another student. If you asked different people, add your results to his/hers. What did most people believe in? What did fewest people believe in? Present your results like this.

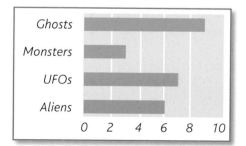

Ghosts

Monsters

UFOs

Aliens

0   2   4   6   8   10

Choose one of the stories from this book. Read the story again. Imagine that it happened to you. Are you, for example, Lionel Foyster? He saw the Borley Ghost. Or are you Lonnie Zamora? He saw aliens and a UFO. Write a letter to a friend. Describe what happened to you. How did you feel?

**1** You and your friend see this in a newspaper. You don't believe in aliens but you want the £500. You decide to phone the newspaper and make up a story. Before you phone, make sure you and your friend have got your story right. Make notes below on your story.

## Have you ever met an ALIEN?

If you have, we would like to meet you! **£500** for your **TRUE** story!
Telephone Alan or Sue at the *Taton Post* on 8892-661235.

When? .............................................................
..................................................................................
..................................................................................

Where? ............................................................
..................................................................................

What happened? ...........................................
..................................................................................
..................................................................................
..................................................................................

How did it end? .............................................
..................................................................................
..................................................................................
..................................................................................
..................................................................................

**2** Work in pairs and practise this telephone conversation.

**Student A:** Telephone the newspaper and ask for Alan or Sue. Tell them that you and your friend have met an alien. Be ready to answer a few questions about your alien meeting!

**Student B:** Imagine that you are Alan or Sue. Speak to the caller and ask a few general questions. Then arrange a time to meet the caller and his/her friend.

**3** **Now work as a class and have a meeting at the newspaper office.**

| Students A and B: | You are the people who telephoned the newspaper office. You say you have met aliens. The other students are going to question you about your story. They want to be sure that your story is TRUE! They will question you one at a time. So make sure you know your story very well! |

| All other students: | You are going to ask questions first to Student A, alone, and then to Student B, alone. You can ask each of them no more than twenty questions. Ask each student the same questions. Do they give the same answers? Is their story true? Make notes below. |

Student A's answers

...........................................................
...........................................................
...........................................................
...........................................................
...........................................................
...........................................................
...........................................................
...........................................................
...........................................................
...........................................................
...........................................................
...........................................................
...........................................................
...........................................................
...........................................................
...........................................................
...........................................................
...........................................................

Student B's answers

...........................................................
...........................................................
...........................................................
...........................................................
...........................................................
...........................................................
...........................................................
...........................................................
...........................................................
...........................................................
...........................................................
...........................................................
...........................................................
...........................................................
...........................................................
...........................................................
...........................................................
...........................................................

**4** You have finished questioning Student A and Student B. Perhaps you believed their story. Perhaps you thought it was untrue. Write a report for the newspaper.

The people

What (they say) happened

True story or not?

Ending